The Incarcerated Investor

A Guide on How to Start Investing While Incarcerated

Authored and Compiled by: J. B. Louden MBA/TM
Book Cover Design by: Rae at Turning Point Virtual Office Services

Distributed by: Future Freedom LLC Rathdrum, ID

ISBN-13: 978-1-7371665-0-4

Get more information at:
www.futurefreedomllc.com

1st printed Edition 2021

Disclaimer:

Mr. Louden endeavors to supply sound information, opinion, and advice based on publicly available information from sources believed to be reliable and from personal experiences. Future Freedom LLC, the author, and their affiliates specifically disclaims any liability, loss, or risk, personal or otherwise, which is incurred as consequence, directly or indirectly, of the use of any application of any content of this book. You should be aware of the real risk of loss in following any strategy or investment. Strategies or investments discussed may fluctuate in price and value. Investors may get back less than invested. Investment strategies mentioned in this book may not be suitable for you. This material does not take into account your particular investment objectives, financial situation, or needs and is not necessarily intended as a recommendation appropriate for you. You must make an independent decision regarding investments or strategies. Before acting on any information from this book you should consider whether it is suitable for your particular circumstances and consider seeking advice from a financial or investment advisor. Mr. Louden's statements and opinions are subject to change without notice. Mr. Louden and his affiliates do not guarantee any specific outcome or profit.

TABLE OF CONTENTS

Introduction

Like many, I am one of 2.5 million people in America warehoused in a prison system someplace. The purpose of this book series is to help educate the incarcerated population across America. Letting the masses know that they can help themselves by creating a path of financial stability for when and if they release back to society. For those that may not have a release date I am sorry, but that does not mean that you cannot take advantage of the positive steps and potential profits from investing while incarcerated. This Series not only will help the incarcerated population but also encourage the average person not behind bars to take that step to start investing, because if an incarcerated individual can achieve success you as a free person have a much easier time to do the same. I hope that the incarcerated people and all Americans across our nation take the step to achieve more wealth by investing.

Politicians across America along with the officials within the walls of the department of corrections continue to mislead the public around the U.S. regarding the help and reform they provide the incarcerated population when it comes to preparing for release back into society. There are very few if any programs within DOC to help the incarcerated person release back into society with one foot ahead or with the ability to be financially prepared. The DOC inhibits and destroys any positive step's an incarcerated person takes to achieve success while incarcerated.

Thousands of men and women walk out the DOC doors with nothing buy the clothes donated to them. These men and women many times release back to young families and conditions that they are not prepared for financially with nothing but an uphill battle. There are states that mandate that the parolee pay a fee every time they report to their parole officer. They may also need to pay for court ordered classes, restitution still owed, housing, food, clothing, and transportation just to name a few. DOC and society just open the prison door and say "Good Luck", with very little preparation or guidance.

I am not telling you this in order to make you depressed. I am telling you this because you are living it and have the opportunity to change your future situation. It's time for men and women across America to take the first positive step and understand that there is an opportunity to start a path to financial success towards their release.

With the help of a trusted family member or friend incarcerated people can start investing and watch their money grow and work for them while incarcerated. Don't be discouraged if you don't have someone that can assist you. You still have the ability to watch your money grow by using a DRIP Transfer Agent account, which you can set up right from your housing unit. I will discuss what a DRIP account is further in this book. Some incarcerated people have a saving account on the streets. But those savings accounts typically only pay you 0.25 of 1% annually on the money you put into the account, they may pay a little more or a little less depending on your bank. But then you have to remember that some of them charge you a fee to maintain the account so you may actually be spending more to maintain that account. How sad! But you can change all of that. By making smart educated investment choices, that same incarcerated person could potentially be making 3% - 10% or more monthly or annually on their money. Giving them a better financial foundation for their future release.

I am not saying that those results are a guarantee for everyone but there is that possibility. Your financial investments are your choices. There are always risks when investing, that is why you always need to do your homework on every company you invest in.

With this book series "The Incarcerated Investor" I will give you information on how I personally set up an individual brokerage account utilizing a power of attorney. This is something I personally accomplished, and believe anyone can do with patients and diligence. Again if you don't have a trusted person to give power of attorney to, you can still invest using a DRIP Transfer Agent. You can set up those accounts directly.

Some companies will accept your power of attorney document, others may want their own specific power of attorney form that can be filled out by you, notarized and sent to your POA. Some financial institutions also require a Power of Attorney - Affidavit and Indemnification form. This form is specifically for your POA to fill out and have notarized, which states that they are who they say they are.

I will go over some information on a few companies that I have researched. If you have other questions you can have your people go to any of the company websites. I will do the best I can to provide as much information as I can, but remember these companies can change fees and charges at any time. It is your responsibility to check with those companies.

The other guides provide investment terminology, and how to do analysis of a company before investing. Don't worry the math skills needed are very simple. Knowing and understanding investment terminology is beneficial to you and knowing how to calculate and evaluate a company before investing is going to be the smartest thing you can do before you put your money into a company. Yes, knowledge is power, but knowledge can be profits too!

Who Can Invest

Anyone can invest in any company that has gone public on the stock exchange markets. There are a lot of Americans that don't know how to get started and they think that they can't invest because they don't have thousands of dollars. Needing thousands of dollars to start investing is a myth. As you read and understand terminology and the process to start an account you will get excited to start doing some analysis of companies. You will understand how to make calculated investment choices and become a confident incarcerated investor, who watches their money grow. Remember I said you don't need thousands to start, I didn't. You can start with as little as $25 to $50. Most companies have adopted the practice of allowing fractional shares in company stocks, anyone can put $50.00 into a Tesla or Apple stock and watch it grow. I personally started with $50.00 each in Google and Amazon. Both companies were in the thousands of dollars for one share when I bought in. But I still bought in and I still make money on my $50.00 investment. You can too!

Step One - Protect yourself and your POA

You are already incarcerated so don't make things worse. Legally protect yourself and your power of attorney. Before you have an account opened in your name online, you need to fill out and notarize a power of attorney. Specifically, a financial power of attorney. Make sure you do not sign your power of attorney until you are standing in front of your notary, they have to witness you sign the document. Once you have your POA notarized you want to make sure you keep a copy of it for yourself if you feel you can safely keep it with you, and send it to the person you have designated as your Power of Attorney.

*** NOTE: Make sure your POA document states that they have the power to open and close financial services and investment accounts along with the ability to file and prepare state and federal taxes for you. I do not guarantee that your POA will be accepted by any financial institution. I have had it accepted and rejected; each institution has their own rules. I will provide a general Durable Power of Attorney form outline. It is your responsibility to understand what a Durable Power of Attorney is and how it is used. Remember that the POA stays in effect until you cancel it. ***

I have known people who have used their mother, father, sibling, aunts, uncles, grandparents, cousins, or friends to set up a power of attorney. It is really who you trust. Make sure you have a conversation with the person you want to have as your POA to make sure they are willing to assist you in getting started. Make sure your POA has the notarized document in hand before you move forward in opening any financial accounts. I do not take any responsibility nor do any of my distributors or affiliates regarding your actions when using any of the forms, opinions, or outlines provided. All these steps are my own personal experiences on how I set up my investment account to start my financial foundation for when I release. If the company you decide to go with declines your POA find out what the reason is and modify your POA to meet the wording and standard they need, get it notarized and resend it to your POA. I personally have had to redo a POA document 3 times to meet the standard and wording for a financial institution to accept my POA.

Step Two - Which Company?

There are several companies you can use to start an individual brokerage account. I will do a short overview of a few companies here. Just a reminder some companies will accept a copy of your financial POA document, some will want their own POA document filled out, notarized and sent to them. If they do want their own POA document it is typically because their POA document describes in detail what your power of attorney has the ability to do within your account. Things like being able to only do trading or unlimited authority, which is not only trading but also withdraw and wire money, make changes or designation of beneficiaries among other things. Like I stated prior companies will most likely want a power of attorney - affidavit and indemnification form. Again, this form is for your POA to fill out themselves and have notarized. This is specifically for the POA to prove to the financial institution they are who they say they are. These documents will assist you in making them your attorney-in-fact for your financial accounts.

Now let's take a quick look at a few companies and what they provide. This list is in no particular order.

Fidelity

Website: www.fidelity.com
Mailing Address:
Fidelity Investments
Po Box 28016
Albuquerque, NM 87125-8016

Account Details:

- Management / Annual Fees
  - $0 on accounts less than $10,000
  - $3.00 a month on accounts with balances of $10,000 - $50,000
  - $0.35% on account balances with more than $50,000
- Buy and sell stocks and ETF's commission free
- Advisory service – Yes
- Zero commission on treasury bond trade
- Allows fractional trading on all stocks
  - Customers can pay as little as $1.00
- Also allows partial trading on ETF's
- Brings IPO offerings to clients – Yes
- Mutual Funds - Yes - 3,000+ offered
- International exchanges available - Yes - 45 offered
- Options Trading – Yes
  - No Base Commissions
  - Contract fees vary
- Financial services available
  - Savings
  - Checking
  - Money Market

Note: I do not recommend options trading for incarcerated people that do not have any experience in this area of stock trading or if they do not have an experienced investor working on their behalf.

Fidelity has an educational tools area for those that are new to investing. I do recommend having your POA utilize this area to learn and understand the tools available.

Also, for those incarcerated that want to send money directly to Fidelity to fund their accounts you can send your state issued checks to:

Fidelity Brokerage Services LLC
Po Box 77001
Cincinnati, OH 45277-0003

**Note: When you fill out your institutional form to have a check cut make sure you put "Deposit {Your name and Account #} in the "To" or "Pay to the Order of" section that will be filled out to Fidelity". **

Charles Schwab

Website: www.schwab.com
Mailing Address:
Charles Schwab & Co,. Inc.
El Paso Operations Center
Po Box 982600
El Pasa, TX 79998-2600

- Management / Annual Fees
    - $0 on Robo portfolios
- $0.14% for underlying expenses
- Buy and sell stocks and ETF's commission free
- Advisory service - Yes - on accounts with min of $5,000
- Zero commission on treasury bond trade
- Allows fractional trading on all stocks listed on S&P 500
    - $5.00 Minimum
- Mutual funds - Yes - 4,000+ offered
    - No sales charge or transaction fee

- Options Trading - Yes
    - No base commissions
    - Contract fees vary

Interactive Brokers (IBKR)
Website: www.interactivebrokers.com
Mailing Address:
Po Box 7579
Greenwich, Connecticut 06836-7579

- Management / Annual Fees
    - Varies from 0.08% - 1.5%
- Buy and sell stocks and ETF's commission free
- Advisory service - Yes - on accounts with a min of $100.00
- Varying fees on treasury bond trades
- Allows fractional trading on almost any stock
    - Shares as little as $0.01
- Mutual funds - Yes - 4,000+ offered
- International exchanges available - Yes - 79 offered
- Options trading - Yes
    - No base commissions
    - Contract fees vary
- Corporate bonds (secondary market) - 26,000 available
- Tax exempt bonds (secondary market) - 992,000 available

TD Ameritrade
Website: www.tdameritrade.com
Mailing Address:
Po Box 2789
Omaha, NE 68103-2789

- Management / Annual fees

- Varies from 0.35% - 0.42%
- Buy and sell stocks and ETF's commission free
- Advisory service - Yes - on accounts with a min $5,000
- Zero commissions on treasury bond trades
- Mutual funds - Yes - 4,000+ offered
- Options Trading - Yes
    - No base commissions
    - Contract fees vary
- Tax exempt bonds (secondary market) - 76,000 available

E*Trade

Website: www.etrade.com

Mailing Address:

Po Box 484
Jersey City, NJ 07303-0484

- Management / Annual fees
    - Varies 0.35% - 0.42%
- Buy and sell stocks and ETF's commission free
- Advisory service - Yes - on accounts with a min $500
- Zero commission on treasury bond trades
- Mutual funds - Yes - 3,000+
- Options Trading - Yes
    - No base commissions
    - Contract fees vary
- Corporate bond (secondary market) - 25,000 available

**NOTE: These brokerage providers may change their fees and services make sure you have your people verify any changes that they may have done. **

Now that you have decided which company you want to establish an account with and your power of attorney has your POA document in hand you can have them go online and create your individual brokerage account for you. I recommend that your POA set up an email account specifically for you in order to have any and all your financial information sent to. Also have them get a composition book in order to write down emails, account information, questions anything important pertaining to your accounts. One more important point, when they are setting up your account you should be on the phone with them so you can answer any questions, they may have during the set up. For example, they will need your social security number. You should have all documentation sent to your power of attorney's address for security reasons. If you want copies of anything you can always have them send you a copy. Don't get frustrated this process can be somewhat cumbersome for some people, be patient with them and the process, remember they are helping you to start a positive financial foundation for your future.

Step Three: Make Contact

Once your account has been created wait 24-48 hours and then have your power of attorney call the company and let them know that they are your power of attorney and need access to your account. In my case my power off attorney was very up front with them and let them know that I had been incarcerated and that they were my POA and needed access to my account in order to maintain my account and make investments for me until my release. The company that I use was very helpful and friendly to my power of attorney, they walked my POA through what was needed and where to send documents. Your POA will need to make sure they take good notes when talking to them so they know where to send information.

My POA sent a copy of my power of attorney document to my company and they also requested the affidavit of indemnification form they had on their website. Once my POA filled out the indemnification form they sent all documents to the address provided by the company. The company I went with told my POA to wait about 10 business days, which allowed the documents to get to the company and then for them to approve the documents and to make the necessary changes to their system for my POA to have access. Once that week was up my POA called them back and they then walked my POA through the process to log into my account and fund it and start making investments and trades on my behalf.

SUCCESS!

**Note: Make sure your POA verifies all addresses and what documents need to be sent were. Your company may have different addresses for different documents. Also make sure your POA sends copies of the documents not the originals. **

Once my POA was able to get into my account I was able to send my power of attorney money in order to fund my account. My POA was able to initially fund my account with their savings account. Their account is only used to put money into your account it is a one time transaction and should not be set up as a permanent link.

Some companies also provide banking services such as money market accounts, checking and savings accounts. If your company provides these services you may be able to establish a savings account through them. You may not need this now, but at least you know its available on release. By establishing a savings account now, you will be able to send money to your own account for deposit and your POA will be able to transfer more money to your investment account for trading and investing.

I have seen people just send money to their POA and their POA just uses their own account for funding your investment account. This will really depend on what your POA is comfortable with doing. This does not allow them to link your account to theirs in order to make money withdrawals. If you and your POA agree to do that they need to download your companies wire transfer account document. Your POA needs to take that document to their bank and have it signed and notarized by them. The financial institution (their bank) has to do the notary in order for them to establish a link between their personal account and your investment account, for purposes of withdrawals. Most savings and checking accounts require a person to have a valid state issued ID, which is something we as incarcerated individuals don't have. It is possible to have a checking and saving account set up with your POA document though. I have done it. I am currently looking into different financial institutions that provide services to the incarcerated population. If you know of any please send us a letter so that we can reach out to them and also pass the word on to others around the nation in the Incarcerated Investor Newsletter.

DRIP Transfer Agents (DRIP Accounts)

A DRIP account is another route an incarcerated individual can take to start saving for their financial future. I am including this option for those of us inside the prison system that do not have any individual on the outside. These accounts can be easy to establish because there is no need for a power of attorney, you can do it all from your institution and housing unit. There are several companies that provide this service. Each company services different stocks so you may have to open several accounts depending on which stocks you may want to invest in. We will list them here along with the company stocks they provide services to. Remember that these company lists can change because of the fast pace of the stock market, so it would be wise to reach out to each company you choose regarding any specific company you may be interested in, to make sure they still service that company. These companies are not listed in any particular order:

Broadridge Corporate Issuer Solutions
Direct Stock Purchase Plan
Po Box 1342
Brentwood, NY 11717-0718

Website: www.broadridge.com
Phone: (877) 830-4936

Alternate Mailing Address:
Broadridge Shareholder Services
1155 Long Island Avenue
Edgewood, NY 11717-8309

Company Listings.

Consumer Discretionary:
Best Buy Company Inc. (BBY)
Collectors Universe Inc. (CLCT)
Walt Disney Co. (DIS)

Consumer Staples:
Kellogg Company (K)
Lancaster Colony Corp. (LANC)
Sysco Corporation (SYY)

Financials:
Ameriprise Financial Inc. (AMP)
Berkshire Hills Bancorp (BHLB)
Chubb Limited (CB)
First Defiance Financial Corp. (FDEF)
Morgan Stanley (MS)
Universal Financial Corp. (UVSP)
Webster Financial Corp. (WBS)

Industrials:
CSX Corp. (CSX)
Curtiss-Wright Corp. (CW)
Deere & Company (DE)
Eaton Corp. (ETN)
Gorman-Rupp Co. (GRC)
Illinois Tool Work Inc. (ITW)

Material:
Air Products & Chemicals Inc. (ADP)
Avery Dennison Corp. (AVY)
Sealed Air Corp. (SEE)
Universal Corp. (UVV)
West Pharmaceutical Serv. Inc. (WST)

Utilities:

CenterPointe Energy (CNP)
Connecticut Water Service Inc. (CTWS)
Dominion Energy Inc. (D)
Middlesex Water Company (MSEX)
New Jersey Resources Corp. (NJR)
RGC Resource Inc. (RGCO)
York Water Company (YORW)

Computershare
Attn: Shareholder Services
Po Box 505000
Louiseville, KY 40233-5000

Website: www.computershare.com
Phone: (800) 446-2617 - Investor Services

Company Listings.

Consumer Discretionary:

ABM Industries Inc. (ABM)
Borg Warner Inc. (BWA)
Brunswick Corp. (BC)
Buckle Inc. (BKE)
Callaway Golf Co. (ELY)
Casey's General Store Inc. (CASY)
Cash America International Inc. (CSH)
Cass Information Systems Inc. (CASS)
Cooper Tire & Rubber Company (CTB)
Domino's Pizza Inc. (DPZ)
E.W. Scripps Co. A (SSP)
Federal Signal Corp. (FSS)
Foot Locker Inc. (FL)

Ford Motor Company (F)
Genuine Parts Co. (GPC)
Hanesbrands Inc. (HBI)
Harley-Davidson Inc. (HOG)
Hasbro Inc. (HAS)
Home Depot (the) Inc. (HD)
Interpublic group of Co. Inc. (IPG)
J.C. Penny Company Inc. (JCP)
Kelly Services Inc. A (KELYA)
Lowe's Companies Inc. (LOW)
LSI Industries Inc. (LYTS)
Macy's Inc. (M)
Manpower Group Inc. (MAN)
Marriott International Inc. A (MAR)
Mattel Inc. (MAT)
McDonald's Corp. (MCD)
Meritor Inc. (MTOR)
NewYork Times Co. A (NYT)
Newell Brands Inc. (NWL)
Nike Inc. B (NKE)
OshKosh Corp. (OSK)
R.R. Donnelley & Sons Co. (RRD)
Sotheby's (BID)
Starbucks Corp. (SBUX)
Superior Industries International Inc. (SUP)
Tiffany & Company (TIF)
VF Corp (VFC)
Whirlpool Corp. (WHR)
Yum! Brands Inc. (YUM)

Consumer Staples:

Agilysys Inc. (AGYS)
Altria Group Inc. (MO)
Andersons (the) Inc. (ANDE)
Avon Products Inc. (AVP)

Boston Beer Co. (the) (SAM)
Brown-Forman Corp. A (BF.A)
Brown-Forman Corp. B (BF.B)
Campbell Soup Co. (CPB)
Church & Dwight Co. Inc. (CHD)
Clorox Company (the) (CLX)
Coca - Cola Company (the) (KO)
Colgate-Polmolive Company (CL)
Costco Wholesales Corporation (COST)
Estee Lauder Companies Inc. (ESS)
Flowers Foods Inc. (FLO)
Hershey Company (the) (HSY)
J.M. Smucker Co. (the) (SJM)
Keurig Dr. Pepper Inc. (KDP)
Libbey Inc. (LBY)
Monsanto Company (MON)
Pepsi Co. Inc. (PEP)
Phillip Morris International Inc. (PM)
Proctor & Gamble Co. (PG)
Sanderson Farms Inc. (SAFM)
Tyson Foods Inc. (TSN)

Energy:

Anadarko Petroleum Corp. (APC)
Chesepeake Utilities Corp. (CPK)
Chevron Corp. (CVX)
Conoco Phillips (COP)
EQT Corp. (EQT)
Exxon Mobil Corp. (XOM)
Halliburton Company (HAL)
HESS Corp. (HES)
Marathon Oil Corporation (MRO)
Marathon Petroleum Corp. (MPC)
Phillips 66 (PSX)
Tidewater Inc. (TDW)

Williams Co. Inc. (WMB)

Financials:

Aetna Inc. (AET)
AGNC Investment Corp. (AGNC)
American Express Co. (AXP)
Ameris Bancorp (ABCB)
Ameriserv Financial Inc. (ASRV)
Annaly Capital Management Inc. (NLY)
AON PLC (AON)
Arthur J. Gallagher & Co. (AJG)
Astoria Financial Corp. (AF)
Auburn National Bancorp Inc. (AUBN)
Bancorp South Bank (BXS)
Bank of America Corp. (BAC)
Bank of Hawaii Corp. (BOH)
Bank of South Carolina Corp. (BKSC)
Bank Financial Corp. (BFIN)
BB&T Corp (BBT)
Boston Private Financial Holdings (BPFH)
Bridge Bancorp Inc. (BDGE)
Bryn Mawr Bank Corp. (BMTC)
Calamos Asset Mgmt. Inc. (CLMS)
Capital One Financial Corp. (COF)
Century Bancorp Inc. (ICNBKA)
Chemical Financial Corp. (CHFC)
Choice One Financial Services Inc. (COFS)
Citigroup Inc. (C)
Citizens Inc. Class A (CIA)
City Holding Co. (CHCO)
Consumer Bancorp Inc. (CBKM)
Discover Financial Services (DFS)
DNB Financial Corp. (DNBF)
Donegal Group Inc. Class A (DGICA)
Elmira Savings Bank (ESBK)

F&M Bank Corp. (FMBM)
F.N.B. Corp. (FNB)
Farmers National Banc Corp. (FMNB)
FBL Financial Group Inc. (FFG)
Fidelity D&D Bancorp Inc. (FDBC)
Fidelity Southern Corp. (LION)
First Bancorp (FBNC)
First Business Financial Services Inc. (FBIZ)
First Capital Inc. (FCAP)
First Commonwealth Financial Corp. (FCF)
First Community Bancshares Inc. (FCBC)
First Community Corp.(FCCO)
First Financial Bancorp (FFBC)
First Internet Bancorp (INBK)
First Keystone Corp. (FKYS)
First Midwest Bancorp Inc. (FMBI)
First Niles Financial Inc. (FNFI)
Franklin Resources Inc. (BEN)
Genworth Financial Inc. (GNW)
German American Bancorp Inc. (GABC)
Great Southern Bancorp Inc. (GSBC)
Harleysville Financial Corp. (HARL)
Hartford Financial Services Group (HIG)
Huntington Bancshares Inc. (HBAN)
Independent Bank Corp (INDB)
Jones Lang LaSalle Inc. (JLL)
Jonestown Bank & Trust Co. (JNES)
JP Morgan Chase & Co. (JPM)
Juniata Valley Financial Corp (JUVF)
Kemper Corp (KMPR)
Key Corp. (KEY)
LCNB Corp (LCNB)
M&T Bank Corp (MTB)
MB Financial Inc. (MBFI)
Mercantile Bank Corp (MBWM)
Mid Penn Bancorp Inc. (MPB)

Mid South Bancorp Inc. (MSC)
Morningstar Inc. (MORN)
Nelnet Inc. (NNI)
New York Community Bancorp Inc. (NYCB)
Old Point Financial Corp. (OPOF)
Peapack Gladstone Financial Corp (PGC)
Penns Woods Bancorp Inc. (PWOD)
People's United Financial Inc. (PBCT)
People's Bancorp of NC Inc. (PEBK)
Perpetual Federal Savings Bank (PFOH)
PNC Financial Services Group (PNC)
Prosperity Bancshares Inc. (PB)
QNB Corp (QNBC)
Regions Financial Corp (RF)
Renasant Corp (RNST)
Republic Bancorp Inc. (RBCAA)
RA International Group PLC (RAI)
S&P Global Inc. (SPGI)
SB Financial Group Inc. (SBFG)
Shore Bancshares Inc. (SHBI)
State Auto Financial Corp. (STFV)
Sterling Bancorp (STL)
Stewart Information Serv. Corp. (STC)
Stifel Financial Corp. (SF)
Stock Yards Bancorp Inc. (SYBT)
Suntrust Banks Inc. (STI)
Taubman Centers Inc. (TCO)
TCF Financial Corp. (TCF)
Towne Bank (TOWN)
TRICO Bancshares (TCBK)
Trustco Bank Corp NY (TRST)
U.S. Bancorp (USB)
UMB Financial Corp. (UMBF)
Umpqua Holdings Corp. (UMPQ)
Union Bancshares Inc. (UBSH)
United Bancshares Inc. (UBOH)

United Bankshares Inc.(UBSI)
United Community Financial Corp. (UCFC)
United Fire Group Inc. (UFCS)
Unity Bancorp Inc. (UNTY)
UNUM Group (UNM)
Wayne Savings Bancshares Inc. (WAYN)
Wesbanco Inc. (WSBC)
Westamerica Bancorp (WABC)

Health Care:

Abbott Laboratories (ABT)
Baxter International Inc. (BAX)
Becton Dickinson & Co. (BDX)
Cigna Corp. (CI)
Johnson & Johnson (JNJ)
Meridian Bio Science Inc. (VIVO)
Owens & Minor Inc. (OMI)
PerkinElmer Inc. (PKI)
Pfizer Inc. (PFE)
Psychemedics Corp. (PMD)
Quest Diagnostics Inc. (DGX)
Zoetis Inc. (ZTS)

Information Technology:

Cisco Systems Inc. (CSCO)
Corning Inc. (GLW)
Herman Miller Inc. (MLHR)
Intel Corp. (INTC)
International Business Machines (IBM)
Motorola Solutions Inc (MSA)
Qualcomm Inc. (QCOM)
Spire Inc. (SR)
Staples Inc. (SPLS)

Texas Instruments Inc. (TXN)
Xerox Corp. (XRX)
Yahoo! Inc. (YHOO)

Industrials:

AAR Corp. (AIR)
Albany International Class A (AIN)
Applied Industrial Tech (AIT)
Boeing Co.(the) (BA)
Caterpillar Inc. (CAT)
Dover Corporation (DOV)
Emerson Electric Co. (EMR)
FEDEX Corp. (FDX)
GATX Corp (GATX)
Goodyear Tire & Rubber (GT)
Greif Inc (GEF)
Harris Corp (HRS)
Harsco Corp (HSC)
Hill-Rom Holdings Inc. (HRC)
Idex Corp (IEX)
Ingersoll-Rand PLC (IR)
Lockheed Martin Corp. (LMT)
Manitowoc Co. Inc. (MTW)
Masco Corp (MAS)
Nordson Corp (NDSN)
Northrop Grumman Corp. (NOC)
Snap-On Incorporated (SNA)
Stanley Black & Decker Inc. (SWK)
Twin Disc Inc. (TWIN)
Union Pacific Corp (UNP)
United Parcel Service Inc. (UPS)
United Technologies Corp. (UTL)
Waste Management Inc. (WM)

Material:

Acuity Brands Inc. (AYI)
Aerojet Rocketdyne Holdings (AJRD)
AGNICO-Eagle Mines Ltd (AEM)
AK Steel Holdings Corp (AKS)
Ball Corp (BLL)
Baker Hughes (BHGE)
Barnes Group Inc. (B)
Carlisle Companies Inc. (CSL)
Clearwater Paper Corp. (CLW)
Crane Company (CR)
DowDuPont Inc. (DWDP)
Ecolab Inc. (ECC)
Ferro Corp. (FOE)
Freeport-McMoran Inc. (FCX)
International Paper (IP)
Linde Plc. (LIN)
Louisiana - Pacific Corporation (LPX)
McDermott International Inc. (MDR)
Omnova Solutions Inc. (OMN)
PPG Industries Inc. (PPG)
SIFCO Industries (SIF)
Southern Copper Corp. (SCCO)
Steel Dynamics Inc.(STLD)
Tredegar Corp. (TG)
USG Corp. (USG)
Vulcan Materials Co. (VMC)
W.R. Grace& Co. (GRA)
Weyerhaeuser Company (WY)

Telecommunications:

Alaska Comm. System Group.(ALSK)
AT&T Inc. (T)
Century Link Inc. (CTL)

Frontier Communications Corp. (FTR)
Sprint Corp. (S)
Telephone & Data Systems Inc. (TDS)
Verizon Communications Inc. (VZ)
Windstream Holdings Inc. (WIN)

Utilities:

American Electric Power (AEP)
American States Water (AWR)
Aqua America Inc. (WTR)
Artesian Resources Corp A (ARTNA)
Avista Corp (AVA)
California Water Service Group (CWT)
Consolidated Edison Inc. (ED)
Eversource Energy (ES)
Great Plains Energy Inc. (GXP)
Idaho Independent Bank (IIBK)
Martin Midstream Partners LP (MMLP)
MGE Energy Inc. (MGEE)
Nextera Energy Inc. (NEE)
NiSource Inc.(NI)
Northwestern Corp. (NWE)
OGE Energy Corp (OGE)
Pinnacle West Capital Corp (PNW)
PNM Resource Inc. (PNM)
South Jersey Industries Inc. (SJI)
UGI Corp (UGI)
Unitil Corporation (UTL)
WEC Energy Group Inc. (WEC)

Real Estate:

Avalonbay Communities Inc. (AVB)
Boston Properties Inc. (BXP)

Brandywine Realty Trust (BDN)
CBL & Associates Properties Inc. (CBL)
CYS Investments Inc. (CYS)
DCT Industrial Trust Inc. (DCT)
DDR Corp (DDR)
EPR Properties (EPR)
Equity Residential (EQR)
Essex Property Trust Inc. (ESS)
First Industrial Realty Trust Inc. (FR)
Getty Realty Corp. (GTY)
Kilroy Realty Corp. (KRL)
Lexington Realty Trust (LXP)
Macerich Company (MAC)
Mack-Cali Realty Corp. (CLI)
MFA Financial Inc. (MFA)
National Health Investors (NHI)
Omega Health Investors Inc. (OHI)

EQ Share Owner Services
Mailing Address:
Po Box 64874
St. Paul, MN 55164-0874

Website: www.shareowneronline.com
Phone: 1-800-468-9716 - Shareowner Relations Department

Note: A list of plans administered by EQ is available at their website under "invest in plan".

Consumer Distrectionary:

Careles Inc. (CAL)
CBS Corporation Class A (Voting) (CBS.A)
CBS Corporation Clsss B (non-voting) (CBS)

Chemed Corp. (CHE)
Comcast Corp. Class A (CMCSA)
CVS Health Corp. (CVS)
Daren Restaurants (DRI)
Dollar General Corp. (DG)
Gannett Company Inc. (GCI)
HNI Corp. (HNI)
Kohl's Corp (KSS)
Marcus Corp. (the) (MCS)
Omnicom Group Inc. (OMC)
Polaris Industries Inc. (PII)
Southwest Airlines Company (LUV)
Target Corp. (TGT)
Viacom Inc. (VIA)
Walgreens Boot Alliance Inc.(WBA)

Consumer Staples:

American Greetings Corp. A (AM)
Brystol-Myers Squibb Co. (BMY)
ConAgra Foods Inc. (CAG)
General Mills (GIS)
Hormel Foods Corp. (HRL)
McCormick & Co. Inc. (MKC)
McKesson Corporation (MCK)
Mondelez International Inc. (MDLZ)

Energy:

Apache Corp. (APA)
Ashland Global Holdings Inc. (ASH)
HollyFrontier Corp. (HFC)
National Fuel Gas Company (NFG)
ONEOK Inc. (OKE)

Financials:

Allstate Corp. (ALL)
Associated Banc Corp. (ASB)
Bank of New York Mellon Corp. (BK)
Block H&R Inc. (HRB)
Bok Financial Corp. (the) (BOKF)
Charles Schwab Corp. (the) (SCHW)
Codorus Valley Bancorp Inc. (CVLY)
Comerica Inc. (CMA)
CorLogic Inc. (CLGX)
First American Financial Corp. (FAF)
HMN Financial Inc. (HMNF)
Lincoln National Corp. (LNC)
Marsh & McLennan Companies Inc. (MMC)
Old Republic International Corp. (ORI)
Pennsylvania REIT (PEI)
Peoples Bancorp Inc. (PEBO)
Regency Centers Corp. (REG)
RLI Corp. (RLI)
Selective Insurance Group Inc. (SIGI)
Senior Housing Properties Trust (SNH)
Torchmark Corp. (TMK)
Travelers Companies Inc. (the) (TRV)
United Security Bancshares (UBFO)
Wells Fargo & Company (WFC)

Health Care:

Abbvie Inc. (ABBV)
Eli Lilly & Company (LLY)
Invacare Corp. (IVC)
Medtronic Plc (MDT)
Merck & Company Inc. (MRK)
Industrials:

A.O. Smith Corp. (AOS)
Brady Corp. (BRC)
Cummins Inc. (CMI)
Donaldson Company Inc. (DCI)
Flowserve Corp. (FLS)
General Electric Company (GE)
Graco Inc. (GGG)
Modine Manufacturing Co. (MOD)
Parker-Haannifin Corp. (PH)
Raven Industries Inc. (RAVN)
Rockwell Automation (ROK)
Ryder System Inc. (R)
Tennant Company (TNC)
TORO Corp. (the) (TTC)
Xylem Inc. (XYL)

Materials:

3M Company (MMM)
Albemarle Corp. (ALB)
Bemis Company Inc. (BMS)
Cleveland-Cliffs Inc. (CLF)
H.B. Fuller Company (FUL)
Hawkins Inc. (HWKN)
Honeywell International Inc. (HON)
Johnson Controls International (JCI)
RPM International Inc. (RPM)
Sherwin Williams Co. (SHW)
Timken Co. (the) (TKR)
United States Steel Corp. (X)
Valmont Industries Inc. (VMI)
Worthington Industries Inc. (WOR)

Real Estate:

Duke Realty Corporation (DRE)

HCP Inc. (HCP)
Kimco Realty Corp. (KIM)
UDR Inc. (UDR)
Ventas Inc. (VTR)

Technology:

Automatic Data Processing (ADP)
Diebold Nixorf Inc. (DBD
NCR Corp. (NCR)
Scripps Network Interactive Inc. (SNI)

Utilities:

Allete Inc. (ALE)
Alliant Energy Corp. (LNT)
Black Hills Corp. (BKH)
CMS Energy Corp (CMS)
DTE Energy Co. (DTE)
Edison International (EIX)
Exelon Corporation (EXC)
IDA Corp Inc. (IDA)
MDU Resources Group Inc. (MDU)
One Gas Inc. (OGS)
Otter Tail Corporation (OTTR)
PG&E Corp. (PCG)
PPL Corp. (PPL)
Public Service Enterprise Group. (PEG)
Southern Company (SO)
Southwest Gas Holdings (SWX)
Xcel Energy Inc. (XEL)

American Stock Transfer
Mailing Address:
6201 15th Ave
Brooklyn, NY 11219

Website: www.astfinancial.com
Phone: 800-937-5449 or 800-387-0825
Email: inquiries@astfinancial.com

Consumer Discretionary:

Carriage Services Inc. (CSV)
Carrols Restaurant Group. Inc. (TAST)
Cracker Barrel Old Country Store (CBRL)
Dunkin' Brands Group Inc. (DNKN)
Fiest Restaurant Group Inc. (FRGI)
L Brands Inc. (LB)
Luby's Inc. (LUB)
Spartan Motors Inc. (SPAR)
Strategic Education Inc. (STRA)
Weiss Markets Inc. (WMK)
World Wrestling Entertainment Inc. (WWE)

Consumer Staples:

Coca-Cola Consolidated Inc. (COKE)
Nutraceutical International Corp. (NUTR)
Reliv' International Inc. (RELV)

Energy:

Buckeye Partners LP (BPL)
Occidental Petroleum (OXY)

Financials:

Acadia Realty Trust (AKR)
Arrow Financial Corp (AROW)
Bancorp of New Jersey Inc. (BKJ)
Bar Harbor Bancshares (BHB)
BGC Partners Inc. (BGCP)
C&F Financial Corp. (CFFI)
Camden National Corp (CAC)
Camden Property Trust (CPT)
Capital City Bank Group (CCBG)
Cardinal Financial Corp (CFNG)
Carver Bancorp Inc. (CARV)
Cathay General Bancorp (CATY)
CCFNB Bancorp Inc. (CCFN)
Cedar Realty Trust (CDR)
Chemung Financial Corp. (CHMG)
Cincinnati Financial Corp. (CINF)
Citizen & Northern Corporation (CZNC)
Citizen Holding Corporation (CIZN)
CNB Financial Corporation (CCNE)
Community Bank System Inc. (CBU)
Dime Community Bancshares Inc. (DCOM)
EMC Insurance Group (EMCI)
Emclaire Financial Corp. (EMCF)
Equifax (EFX)
Fauquier Bankshares Inc. (FBSS)
Federal Realty Investment Trust (FRT)
Fifth Third Bancorp (FITB)
First Merchants Corp. (FRME)
Franklin Street Properties (FSP)
Glacier Bancorp Inc. (GBCI)
Hartford Bank (HFBK)
Hawthorn Bancshares Inc. (HWBK)
Horace Mann Educators Corp. (HMN)
Investors Real Estate (IRET)

Jeffersonville Bancorp (JFBC)
Kentucky First Federal Bancorp (KFFB)
Lakeland Bancorp Inc. (LBAI)
Lakeland Financial Corp. (LKFN)
Manulife Financial Corp. (MFC)
Medallion Financial Group (MFIN)
Mid-America Apartment Communities Inc. (MAA)
Middleburg Financial Corp. (MBRG)
Middlefield Band Corp. (MBCN)
Monmouth REIT Corp. (MNR)
National Retail Properties Inc.(NNN)
Northwest Bancshares Inc. (NWBI)
OceanFirst Financial Corp. (OCFC)
Paychex Inc. (PAYX)
People Financial Services Corp. (PFIS)
RAIT Financial Trust Inc. (RASF)
S&T Bancorp Inc. (STBA)
SBT Bancorp Inc. (SBTB)
Sotherly Hotels Inc. (SOHO)
Southwest Georgia Financial Corp. (SGB)
State Street Corp. (STT)
Steuben Trust Co. (SBHO)
Sturgis Bancorp (STBI)
SB One Bancorp (SBBX)
Synovus Financial Corp. (SNV)
Tompkins Financial Corp. (TMP)
Total System Services Inc. (TSS)
Trustmark Corp. (TRMK)
UMH Properties Inc.(UMH)
United Bancorp Inc. (UBCP)
Valley National Bancorp (VLY)
Washington Trust Bancorp Inc.(WASH)
WSFS Financial Corp. (WSFS)

Health Care:

Amgen Inc. (AMGN)
Zimmer Bionet Holdings Inc. (ZBH)

Industrials:

Ametek Inc. (AME)
Badger Meter Inc. (BMI)
Chase Corp. (CCF)
Columbus McKinnon Corp. (CMCO)
La-Z-Boy Inc. (LZB)
Norfolk Southern Corp. (NSC)
Raytheon Company (RTN)
Teleflex Inc. (TFX)
Textron Inc. (TXT)
Woodword Inc. (WWD)

Materials:

A.M. Castle & Co. (CAS)
Arch Coal Inc. (ARCH)
Beazer Homes USA Inc. (BZH)
Carpenter Technology Corp. (CRS)
Eastman Chemical Co.(EMN)
Insteel Industries Inc. (IIIN)
International Flavors & Fragrances (IFF)
Nucor Corp. (NUE)
Peabody Energy Corp. (BTU)
Quaker Chemical Corp. (KWR)

Technology:

Microsoft Corporation (MSFT)
Skyworks Solutions Inc. (SWKS)

Utilities:

American Water Works (AWK)
Atmos Energy Corp. (ATO)
AVX Corp. (AVX)
Consolidated Water Company Ltd. (CWCO)
First Energy Corp. (FE)
Northwest Natural Gas Co. (NWN)
Portland General Electric Co. (POR)
Sempra Energy (SRE)

Continental Stock
Mailing Address:
17 Battery Place
New York, NY 10004

Website: www.continentalstock.com
Phone: 212-509-4000
Email: cstmail@continentalstock.com

Financials:

First of Long Island Corp. (FLIC)
Orrstown Financial Services Inc. (ORRF)
Seacoast Banking Corp. of Florida (SBCF)

Industrials:

Sonoco Products Co. (SON)

All of these companies provide DRIP accounts that you as an incarcerated investor can access and start from your housing unit. This option provides a great opportunity to investing rather than trying to establish an individual brokerage investment account. There are a lot of individuals locked up that do not have someone on the outside to assist them. You can start an account at several DRIP Transfer Agent companies in order to invest in several different stocks. Once you have invested, they will send you a monthly or quarterly report of what you have invested each quarter, along with the dividends you have received from those stocks. Remember to always do your research on any company you plan on investing into. Just because they provide a dividend does not mean they will be a stable company.

Staying Positive and Optimistic

Living in a concrete box with bars and razor wire while enduring ground hog's day over and over again can be tiresome. But remember there are opportunities out there. This is one of them. Invest in order to invest in yourself later on. Look around you how many people do you know in your current situation are optimistic. Not many rights? That's because being optimistic is a rare attribute in people that come into hard situations. We as humans want to be, but society has made our population nervous and scared. Take this opportunity and start building for yourself today. An optimistic person will look for opportunities and move on them, taking a chance. For example when people are in the stock market and they see their stocks falling in price they tend to get nervous and sell, while an optimistic person may look at it as a buying opportunity to get more stock at a better price, which means when it goes up they make more money. It's a bargain, not a loss. But be patient because sometimes a optimistic person can go too far and spend too much. Believing they can get rich quick and go down a road of over extending themselves financially which can be a detriment to their bottom line of investing. So be careful and mindful of your potential investments. We all want to believe there is someone in the stock market with magical powers that can tell us when and where to invest, but it is simply not true.

You have to do your homework and be able to stay positive in down turns, in other words don't let the bears run you over. Because if you turn and run there is going to be a bull waiting to step in and charge forward with your potential profits.

For those of us that are incarcerated the key is to think positive. Keep your optimism in control along with patience. Make sure you weigh the risks with the possible gains. That is what will lead all of us down the road of financial stability. I know I keep pounding it in and saying do your homework and research but it truly is going to be the best thing you do while you invest. My money is important to me, and I don't have a lot of it so I want to make sure it is working the best way it can for me and make the most possible.

I want this book series to help all incarcerated individuals get started with the knowledge of investing and how to. Being able to show the world that you took the opportunity to invest in your future is a positive change. We may not be able to do day trading but there is still that opportunity and potential to invest and hold onto companies that will increase our wealth, making us more money while we are incarcerated. I hope you take this and become an incarcerated investor and walk out the doors of your DOC better and wealthier then when you came in.

Move, adjust and keep records

Even though as an incarcerated investor the easiest plan is to "buy good stocks and hold them long term", there are times when we need to sell those stocks. Just because you bought a stock doesn't mean you are married to it. When you see a company that you own is deteriorating, the product they produce is becoming obsolete, their market share is shrinking, or they have put themselves in an unfavorable position it may be time to sell. Take your profits and move to a more favorable company. Don't be afraid to adjust your portfolio positions. There are a lot of different ways you can play the market. I know one incarcerated investor that invests and once his investment has moved up 30%, he sells and moves to another investment. He is always moving and making changes. I am not saying that this is a good strategy, it works for him and he has people on the streets that can make those moves for him. He enjoys playing risky, I don't. It keeps him engaged and busy researching companies and doing his homework. Its time well spent. Start a portfolio, ride with it for a while, make changes when needed.

It's a good idea to keep good records of what you spent and what your buy in cost is. Yes, the companies you invest through will send you reports on these things also. Buy it will help you learn how to maintain your own financials also. This is a start to being financially stable for your future.

So, start now. Make a list of companies start doing research and evaluating the risks of investing into them. Or choose a few companies and start a DRIP account for long term dividend investing. Either way you are now going to be on your way to becoming an incarcerated investor making a positive change in your life, creating a path of success for your future. I love having the opportunity to show the people in society that we as outcasts (felons) can achieve greatness too.

The next 2 guides will help you understand terminology, and how to do analysis with different strategies. Invest and achieve wealth and stability.

The following example is my personal durable power of attorney document that I have used at several financial institutions.

***Note: Do not sign your power of attorney document until you are sitting in front of your notary. The notary has to witness you signing the document. ***

Everything beyond this point is in my personal POA document.

***** Power of Attorney *****

DURABLE POWER OF ATTORNEY FOR FINANCIAL MANAGEMENT

** Warning ** The powers you grant below continue to be effective should you become disabled or incompetent.

Caution: This is an important legal document and upon proper execution will create a Durable Power of Attorney. This gives the person whom you designate as your attorney-in-fact broad powers to handle your property during your lifetime, which may include powers to mortgage, sell, or otherwise dispose of any real or personal property without advance notice to you or approval by you.

These powers will continue to exist even if you become disabled or incompetent. You DO have the right to terminate or revoke the Power of Attorney and any or all powers granted within at any time up to the incapacity.

This document DOES NOT authorize anyone to make medical or other health care decisions. You may execute a health care proxy (also known as a health care or medical power of attorney) to do this.

If there is anything about this document that you do not understand, you should ask a lawyer to explain it to you.

THIS DURABLE POWER OF ATTORNEY for financial management is given by me, ____(the

"Principal"), presently located at ____ USA, on this __________ day of ____________ (month), ____________(year).

Nature of Power

1. THIS IS A DURABLE POWER OF ATTORNEY and the authority of my Attorney-in-fact shall not terminate if I become disabled or incapacitated.

Previous Power of Attorney,

2. I REVOKE any previous durable power of attorney granted by me.

Attorney-in-fact

3. I APPOINT ______________________ of ____________________ (full address), USA, to act as my Attorney-in-fact.

Successor Attorney-in-fact

4. On the death refusal or inability of __________________ to act or continue to act, I APPOINT ____, of ____(full address), USA, to act in place of ____ as my successor Attorney-in-fact.

My "Attorney-in-fact"

5. I will refer to my Attorney-in-fact and my successor Attorney-in-fact as my "Attorney-in-fact".

Governing Law

6. This document will be governed by the laws of the State of ____________________. Further, my Attorney-in-fact is directed to act in accordance with the laws of the State of ____________________ at any time he or she may be acting on my behalf.

Liability of Attorney-in-fact

7. My Attorney-in-fact will not be liable to me, my estate, my heirs, successors or assigns for any action taken or not taken under this document, except for willful misconduct or gross negligence. A successor Attorney-in-fact will not be liable for acts of a prior Attorney-in-fact.

Effective Date

8. This Power of Attorney will start immediately and will continue not withstanding finding of my mental incapacity or mental infirmity which may occur after my execution of this Power of Attorney.

Powers of Attorney-in-fact

9. My Attorney-in-fact will have the following power(s):

Initials

a. __________ Real Estate Transactions

To deal with any interest I may have in real property and sign all documents on my behalf concerning my interest, including, but not limited to, real property I may subsequently acquire or receive. These powers include, but are not limited to, the ability to:

I. Purchase, sell, exchange, accept as gift, place as security on loans, convey with or without covenants, rent, collect rent,sue for and receive rents, eject and remove tenants or other persons, to pay contest, taxes or assessments, control any legal claim in favor of or against me, partition or consent to partitioning, mortgage, change, lease, surrender, manage or otherwise deal with real estate and any interest therein; and

II. Execute and deliver deeds, transfers, mortgages, charges, leases, assignments, surrenders, releases and other instruments required for any such purpose.

b. __________ Maintain Property and Make Investments

To retain any assets owned by me at the date this Durable Power of Attorney becomes affective, and the power to reinvest those assets in similar investments. In addition, my Attorney-in-fact may invest my assets in any new investments, of his or her choosing, regardless of whether or not they are authorized by any applicable legislation.

c. __________ Banking Transactions

To do any act that I can do through an Attorney-in-fact with a bank or other financial institution. This power includes, but is not limited to, the power to:

I. Open, maintain or close bank accounts (including, but not limited to, personal checking accounts, personal savings accounts, business checking accounts, business savings accounts, and certificates of deposit), brokerage accounts, retirement plan accounts, and other similar accounts with financial institutions;

II. Conduct any business with any banking or financial institution with respect to any of my accounts, including, but not limited to, making deposits and withdrawals, negotiating or endorsing any checks or other instruments with respect to any such accounts, obtaining bank statements, passbooks, drafts, money orders, warrants, and certificates or vouchers payable to me by any person, firm, corporation or political entity;

III. Borrow money from any banking or financial institution if deemed necessary by my Attorney-in-fact, and to manage all aspects of the loan process, including the placement of security and the negotiation of terms;

IV. Perform any act necessary to deposit, negotiate, sell or transfer any note, security, or draft of the United States of America, including U.S. Treasury Securities;

V. Have access to any safe deposit box that I might own, including its contents, and;

VI. Create and deliver any financial statements necessary to or from any bank or financial institution.

d. __________ Business Operating Transactions

To take any action my Attorney-in-fact deems necessary with any business that I may own or have an interest in by doing any act which can be done through an Attorney-in-fact. This power includes, but is not limited to, the power to execute, seal and deliver any instrument; create and open any legal business; participate in any legal business of any kind; execute partnership agreements and amendments; to incorporate, reorganize, consolidate, merge, sell, or dissolve any business; to elect or employ officers, directors and agents; and to exercise voting rights with respect to any stock I may own, either in person or by proxy.

e. __________ Insurance Transactions

To do any act that I can do through an Attorney-in-fact with any insurance policy. This power includes, but is not limited to, the power to pay premiums, start, modify, or terminate policies, manage all cash payouts, borrow from insurers and third parties using insurance policies as collateral, and to change the beneficiaries of any policy before signing of this document, my Attorney-in-fact cannot name himself or herself as a beneficiary of such policy.

f. __________ Claims and Litigation

To institute, maintain, defend, compromise, arbitrate or otherwise dispose of, any and all actions, suits, attachments or other legal proceedings for or against me. This power includes, but is not limited to, the power to appear on my behalf, and the power to settle any claim against me in whichever forum or manner my Attorney-in-fact deems prudent, and to receive or pay any resulting settlement.

g. __________ Tax Matters

To act for me in all matters that affect my local, state and federal taxes and to prepare, sign, and file documents with any governmental body or agency, including, but not limited to, authority to:

I. Prepare, sign and file income and other tax returns with federal, state, local and other governmental bodies, and to receive any refund check; and

II. Obtain information or documents from any government or its agencies, and represent me in all tax matters, including the authority to negotiate, compromise, or settle any matter with such government or agency.

h. __________ Government Benefits

To act on my behalf in all matters that affect my right to allowances, compensation and reimbursements properly payable to me by the government of the United States or any agency or department thereof. This power includes, but is not limited to, the power to prepare, file, claim, defend or settle any claim on my behalf and to receive and manage, as my Attorney-in-fact sees fit, any proceeds of any claim.

i. __________ Retirement Benefits

To act for me and represent my interests in all matters affecting any retirement savings or pension plans I may have. This power includes, but is not limited to, the power to continue contributions, change contribution amounts, change investment strategies and options, move assets to other plans, receive and manage payouts, and add or change existing beneficiaries. My Attorney-in-fact cannot add himself or herself as a beneficiary unless he or she is already a designated beneficiary as of the signing of this document.

j. __________ Family Care

To make whatever expenditures are required for the maintenance, education, benefit, medical care and general advancement of me, my spouse and defendant children, and other persons that I have chosen or which I am legally required to support, any of which may include my Attorney-in-fact. This power includes, but is not limited to, the power to pay for housing, clothing, food, travel and other living costs.

k. __________ Chattel and Goods

To purchase, sell or otherwise deal with any type of personal property I may currently or in the future have an interest in. This includes, but is not limited to, the power to purchase, sell, exchange, accept as gift, place as security on loans, rent, lease, to pay or contest taxes or assessments, mortgage or pledge.

l. __________ Estate Transactions

To do any act that I can do through an Attorney-in-fact with regards to all matters that affect any trust, probate estate, conservatorship, or other fund from which I may receive payment as a beneficiary. This power includes the power to disclaim any interest which might otherwise be transferred or distributed to me from any other person, estate, trust, or other entity, as may be appropriate. However, my Attorney-in-fact cannot disclaim assets to which I would be entitled, if the result is that the disclaimed asset pass directly or indirectly to my Attorney-in-fact or my Attorney-in-fact estate.

m. __________ Living Trust

To transfer any of my assets to the trustee of any revocable trust created by me, if such trust is inexistence at the time of such transfer. This property can include real property, stocks, bonds, accounts, insurance policies or other property.

n. __________ Gift Transactions

To make gifts to my spouse, children, grandchildren, great grandchildren, and other family members on special occasions, including birthdays and seasonal holidays, including cash gifts, and to such other persons with whom I have an established pattern of giving (or if it is appropriate to make such gifts for estate planning and/or tax purposes), in such amounts as my Attorney-in-fact may decide in his or her absolute discretion, having regard to all of the circumstances, including the gifts I made while I was capable of managing my own estate, the size of my estate and my income requirements.

o. __________ Charity Transactions

To continue to make gifts to charitable organizations with whom I have an established pattern of giving (or if it is appropriate to make such gifts for estate planning and/or tax purposes), in such amounts as my Attorney-in-fact may decide in his or her absolute discretion, having regard to all of the circumstances, including the gifts I made while was capable of managing my own estate, the size of my estate and my income requirements.

p. __________ Employ Required Professionals

To appoint and employ any agents, servants, companions, or other persons, including nurses and other health care professionals for my care and the care of my spouse and dependent children, and accountants, attorneys, clerks, workers and others for management, preservation and protection of my property and estate, at such compensation and for such length of time as my Attorney-in-fact considers advisable.

Attorney-in-fact Compensation

10. My Attorney-in-fact will receive no compensation except for the reimbursement of all out of pocket expenses associated with the carrying out of my wishes.

11. Co-Owning of Assets and Mixing of Funds

My Attorney-in-fact may continue to co-own assets and have any funds owned by him or her mixed with my funds to the same extent that the co-owning of assets and mixing of funds existed before operation of this Power of Attorney.

12. Delegation of Authority

My Attorney-in-fact may delegate any authority granted under this document to a person of his or her choosing. Delegation must be in writing and state the extent of the power delegated and the period of time in which the delegation will be effective.

13. Nomination of Guardian or Conservator

In the event that a court decides that it is necessary to appoint a guardian or conservator for me, I hereby nominate my Attorney-in-fact to be considered by the court for appointment to serve as my guardian or conservator, or in any similar representative capacity.

14. Attorney-in-fact Restrictions

This Power of Attorney is not subject to any conditions or restrictions other than those noted above.

15. Notice to Third Parties

Any third party who receives a valid copy of this Power of Attorney can rely on and act under it. A third party who relies on the reasonable representations of my Attorney-in-fact as to a matter relating to a power granted by this Power of Attorney will not incur any liability to the Principal or to the Principal's heirs, assigns, or estate as a result of permitting the Attorney-in-fact to exercise the authority granted by this Power of Attorney up to the point of revocation of this Power of Attorney. Revocation of this Power of Attorney will not be effective as to a third party until the third party receives notice and has actual knowledge of the revocation.

16. Severability

If any part of any provision of this document is ruled invalid or unenforceable under applicable law, such part will be ineffective to the extent of such invalidity only, without in any way affecting the remaining parts of such provisions or the remaining provisions of this document.

17. Acknowledgment

I, ______________________________, being the Principal named in this Durable Power of Attorney hereby Acknowledge:

a. I have read and understand the nature and effect of this Durable Power of Attorney;

b. I recognize that this document gives my Attorney-in-fact broad powers over my assets, and that these powers will continue past the point of my incapacity;

c. I am of legal age in the state of ________________ to grant a Durable Power of Attorney; and

d. I am voluntarily giving this Durable Power of Attorney and recognize that the powers given in this document will become effective as of the date of my incapacity or as specified within.

IN WITNESS WHEREOF I hereunto set my hand and seal at the City of __________________________ in the State of ____________________, this __________________ day of ________________, ___________.

SIGNED

____

(the "Principal")

NOTARY ACKNOWLEDGEMENT

STATE OF ______________________________

COUNTY OF ______________________________

On this ____________ day of ______________, ____________(month), __________________ (year) before me, ______________________________ a Notary Public in and for the State of __________________, personally appeared ____, known or identified to me, (or proved to me on the oath of ______________________), to be the person whose name is subscribed to the within instrument, and acknowledge to me that he/she executed the same.

____

Notary Public Signature

My Commission Expires: ______________________

____

Notary - Affix Stamp Here

Check List:

This check list is for the purpose of utilizing Power of Attorney to establish a brokerage account.

[ ] Speak to several people you trust about starting brokerage account for you and being your POA

[ ] Decide who is going to be your Power of Attorney

[ ] Create your Power of Attorney document

- You may need to have your people send you a blank document or if your institution allows you to create your own you can do that. Some people have hand written the document and had it Notarized, this may work, depending on the financial institution.

[ ] Research the brokerage account provider you are interested in

[ ] Decide on a brokerage account provider

[ ] Mail your signed POA to the person you have chosen as your Power of Attorney

[ ] Have your POA go online and create your brokerage account for you

[ ] Once your account is established wait 24-48 hours and then have your POA call the company and let them know that they are your POA and need access to your account.

- Note: When your POA signs you up for your account I would use their mailing address for purposes of mailing your financial documents to you, for security reasons. You can always have them send you copies of documents if you want them.

- Also have your POA ask for the address that you can send money orders, or institutional checks to in order to fund your account directly if you would like to.

[ ] Start researching different companies you are interested in to invest in.

[ ] Send funds to your POA to have them start funding your account or get your account number to start funding your account yourself

[ ] Be flexible and move when needed to protect your money

[ ] Sit back and watch your money grow!

Congratulations you are now an Incarcerated Investor making money for your future freedom!

Check List: This check list is for purposes of creating a DRIP account through a transfer agent.

[ ] Research a DRIP Account Transfer Agent

- Send letters to the DRIP Agents that you are interested in and ask them for a list of the companies they service along with their enrollment forms.

- You may have a few accounts with different companies because they all service different stocks.

[ ] Fill out the transfer agent applications along with any other documentation they need.

[ ] Send your money with the application if needed.

[ ] Ask question of your DRIP agent they should answer you.

[ ] Look over your statements and watch your money grow.

Congratulations you are now an incarcerated investor investing for your future freedom!

FUTURE FREEDOM LLC

Order The Incarcerated Investor Book Series and Reference Guide Today!

Please fill in the form and send the Book Purchase Order with check or money order to:

Future Freedom LLC.
Po Box 454
Rathdrum, ID 83858

BOOK PURCHASE ORDER FORM

Pre-Order now. Distribution begins Jan 2022.

[ ] Guide to start investing while incarcerated	$27.00
[ ] Guide to basic investor terminology	$27.00
[ ] Guide on how to analyze a company stock	$27.00

Order Now - Updated Q3 2021

[ ] Incarcerated Investor Reference Guide	$37.00

Institution Name:___________________________________

Last Name: ________________**FirstName:**________________

State Issued ID Number:______________________________

Unit/Cell# (If required for Delivery):__________________

Address:____

City:______________**State:**______________**Zip Code:**________

Release Date:________ /________ **(month/year)** [ ] **Life Sentence**

*** Release Date is used for our news letter service. ***

**** Note: We will not refund lost, stolen, rejected, or returned publications. ****

FUTURE FREEDOM LLC

Order The Incarcerated Investor Book Series and Reference Guide Today!

Please fill in the form and send the Book Purchase Order with check or money order to:

Future Freedom LLC.
Po Box 454
Rathdrum, ID 83858

✂- - - - - - - - - - - - - - - - - - - -

BOOK PURCHASE ORDER FORM

Pre-Order now. Distribution begins Jan 2022.

[ ] Guide to start investing while incarcerated	$27.00
[ ] Guide to basic investor terminology	$27.00
[ ] Guide on how to analyze a company stock	$27.00

Order Now - Updated Q3 2021

[ ] Incarcerated Investor Reference Guide	$37.00

Institution Name:____

Last Name: ____________________ **FirstName:**____________________________

State Issued ID Number:____

Unit/Cell# (If required for Delivery):__________________________

Address:____

City:____________________**State:**____________________**Zip Code:**__________

Release Date:__________/__________ **(month/year)** **[ ] Life Sentence**

*** Release Date is used for our news letter service. ***

**** Note: We will not refund lost, stolen, rejected, or returned publications. ****

FUTURE FREEDOM LLC

Order The Incarcerated Investor Book Series and Reference Guide Today!

Please fill in the form and send the Book Purchase Order with check or money order to:

Future Freedom LLC.
Po Box 454
Rathdrum, ID 83858

✂- - - - - - - - - - - - - - - - - - - -

BOOK PURCHASE ORDER FORM

Pre-Order now. Distribution begins Jan 2022.

[ ] Guide to start investing while incarcerated	$27.00
[ ] Guide to basic investor terminology	$27.00
[ ] Guide on how to analyze a company stock	$27.00

Order Now - Updated Q3 2021

[ ] Incarcerated Investor Reference Guide	$37.00

Institution Name:____

Last Name: __________________**FirstName:**______________________

State Issued ID Number:____

Unit/Cell# (If required for Delivery):_____________________________

Address:____

City:_________________**State:**__________________**Zip Code:**_________

Release Date:________ /________ **(month/year)** **[ ] Life Sentence**

*** Release Date is used for our news letter service. ***

**** Note: We will not refund lost, stolen, rejected, or returned publications. ****

FUTURE FREEDOM LLC

Company Reports Service

These company reports provide information regarding company stock prices and company information for the incarcerated investor. These reports have been praised time and time again by the incarcerated investor.

Please fill in the form and send with check or money order to:

Future Freedom LLC c/o Reports Division
Po Box 454
Rathdrum, ID 83858

✂ - - - - - - - - - - - - - - - - - - -

Institution Name:____________________________________

Last Name: __________________**FirstName:**____________________

State Issued ID Number:________________________________

Unit/Cell# (If required for Delivery):________________________

Address:____

City:__________________**State:**__________________**Zip Code:**________

Release Date:________ /________ **(month/year)** [ ] **Life Sentence**

*** Release Date is used for our news letter service. ***

**** Note: We will not refund lost, stolen, rejected, or returned reports. ****

**** $3.00 per report - Maximum of 4 companies / 1 report each per order ****

Company Name	Symbol	$$

Reports Total:	
(+ $3.00 Processing):	+$3.00
Order Total:	

FUTURE FREEDOM LLC

Company Reports Service

These company reports provide information regarding company stock prices and company information for the incarcerated investor. These reports have been praised time and time again by the incarcerated investor.

Please fill in the form and send with check or money order to:

Future Freedom LLC c/o Reports Division
Po Box 454
Rathdrum, ID 83858

✂ -

Institution Name:______________________________________

Last Name: __________________**FirstName:**______________________

State Issued ID Number:_________________________________

Unit/Cell# (If required for Delivery):_________________________

Address:____

City:__________________**State:**__________________**Zip Code:**________

Release Date:_______ /_______ **(month/year)** [ ] **Life Sentence**

*** Release Date is used for our news letter service. ***

**** Note: We will not refund lost, stolen, rejected, or returned reports. ****

**** $3.00 per report - Maximum of 4 companies / 1 report each per order ****

Company Name	Symbol	$$

Reports Total:	________
(+ $3.00 Processing):	+$3.00
Order Total:	________

FUTURE FREEDOM LLC

Company Reports Service

These company reports provide information regarding company stock prices and company information for the incarcerated investor. These reports have been praised time and time again by the incarcerated investor.

Please fill in the form and send with check or money order to:

Future Freedom LLC c/o Reports Division
Po Box 454
Rathdrum, ID 83858

✂ - - - - - - - - - - - - - - - - - - -

Institution Name:____

Last Name: __________________**FirstName:**__________________________

State Issued ID Number:____________________________________

Unit/Cell# (If required for Delivery):___________________________

Address:____

City:__________________**State:**__________________**Zip Code:**________

Release Date:________ /________ **(month/year)**   **[ ] Life Sentence**

*** Release Date is used for our news letter service. ***

**** Note: We will not refund lost, stolen, rejected, or returned reports. ****

**** $3.00 per report - Maximum of 4 companies / 1 report each per order ****

Company Name	Symbol	$$

Reports Total:	
(+ $3.00 Processing):	+$3.00
Order Total:	

Future Freedom and Affiliates

Address: **Future Freedom LLC. P.O. Box 454, Rathdrum, ID 83858**

Website: **www.futurefreedomllc.com**

Facebook: **www.facebook.com/futurefreedomllc**

Email addresses:

services@futurefreedomllc.com - Questions regarding services (please include your name, state identification #, and mailing address)

postcard@futurefreedomllc.com - This email is for friends and family to send your mailing information to Future Freedom in order to receive our mailings.

MAINLINE
PRESS, LLC

Address: PO Box 517
Creswell, OR 97426
Facebook: www.facebook.com/mainlinepressofficial

Instagram: www.facebook.com/mainlinepressofficial

Twitter: www.twitter.com/PressMainline

Email addresses: mainlinepress97501@gmail.com
raemlpllc@gmail.com

Mainline Press New Offerings!

TURNING POINT SERIES

Turning Point - Social Security, Supplemental Benefits, and Veterans Benefits and What You Need to Know While Incarcerated

NOW AVAILABLE ON AMAZON!

Learn the truth about what you are entitle to while incarcerated as well as what you can do to prepare for your release. All new and updated with the most up-to-date information from the new administration. **Only** *$14.99*

Turning Point - Pre-Trial

The truth about the pre-trial process, real world information, tips and tactics to defend yourself, and what they don't want you to know that could save your life.

New Price: *$24.99*

Turning Point - Direct Appeal

A step-by-step guide through the Direct Appeal process and what you need to know to hold your attorney accountable or represent yourself.

Only *$24.99*

Turning Point - Post-Conviction Relief

An in-depth, step-by-step guide through the process that includes: information, terminologies, and the important caselaw necessary to hold your attorney accountable or represent yourself.
New Price: *$24.99*

Turning Point - Habeas Corpus

A comprehensive step-by-step guide to the sometimes confusing Federal Habeas Corpus process. A must read for anyone looking to win their Habeas.

Only *$24.99*

Turning Point – Clemency

An in-depth explanation of the Clemency process with detailed steps that can help you gain your Clemency. Educate yourself and go into this process knowing what you are doing.

Only *$24.99*

RELATIONSHIP SERIES

Parenting From Prison

Only *$14.99*

What You Need To Know About Your Parental Rights While Incarcerated

New Price: *$14.99*

Meaningful Letter And Message Writing

Only *$9.99*

How To Lower Stress And Find Peace With Mindfulness And Meditation

Only *$19.99*

Heartfelt Projects And Gift Ideas That You Can Utilize From Prison

Only *$9.99*

REENTRY SERIES

How To Make Your Parole/Probation Officer Your Ally

New Price: *$14.99*

Self Monitoring To Protect Yourself While On Post- Prison Supervision

Only *$14.99*

Job Search And Felon Friendly Employment

Only *$9.99*

Non- Extradition Countries And What You Need To Know About Them

Only *$14.99*

How To Build A Business Plan That Can Help You Get SBA Funding

Only *$19.99*

How To Build A Marketing Plan That Can Help You Get SBA Funding

Only *$19.99*

INFORMATION SERIES

The Truth About Bar Complaints And How To File Them

Only *$14.99*

How To File A Complaint Against A Private Investigator, Polygraph Examiner, Police/Correctional Officer, Parole/Probation Officer

New Price: *$14.99*

How To Best Utilize Your Friends And Family Resources While Incarcerated

Only *$9.99*

How To Make A Durable Power Of Attorney And Why It's Important During Your Incarceration

Only *$14.99*

How To Protect Your Money While Incarcerated With A Self- Directed IRA

Only *$19.99*

Project Mainline National Prison Advocacy Directory

Only *$9.99*

MAINLINE PRESS, LLC
AUGUST 2021

A FEW QUICK REMINDERS

August is:
National Black Business Month
Happiness Happens Month
National Immunization Awareness Month

August 1st: B.C. Day (Canada)

August 15th: Assumption (Church Festival of Virgin Mary)

FROM THE EDITOR

When I was first arrested, I literally knew nothing about the criminal justice system. Like most others in the general public, I thought I had a general idea of how things worked but, as it turns out, the few episodes of COPS or CSI that I caught didn't provide me an education or a working knowledge about the system. Years later and looking back, I can see that this is truly one of the larger issues with our broken criminal justice system. People in the public think that they know how it works when in all actuality, they have no idea how it really works. In fact, most of them only find out the truth after they are affected by it personally and when they do, they're appalled by it. Guilty, innocent, or in between, most of us have families who are sickened by what has happened to their loved ones. It could be the lack of police accountability, lack of an investigation, lack of adequate representation, or the unfair things that the prosecutor was allowed to do in the courtroom. These are all things that most people earn an education from the hard way. Given the current social climate of this country, it's not a stretch to think that the public would be up in arms if they knew how things really work. Our system, however, is designed to keep its dirtiest secrets, just that. Secrets.

An example of this is found in the Settlement Conference. When I was in county jail I had no idea what a Settlement Conference was. My public defender provided me no information about it or even notice that I would have one and there was a total void of information about it. In fact, at that time, there

PAGE 1

Check Out The Project Mainline Newsletter!

This monthly 10-page newsletter is packed with the information most important to incarcerated people and their loved ones. Includes Information about changing laws, Stories on Prison Reform, New Inmate Service Company Reviews, Tips on Business and Money while incarcerated, and much much more. We offer all of this at below our price of printing and postage to keep you informed about things you need to know about. Order today. **Only:** *$9.99* per year!

To order simply make a list of the titles that you would like sent to you. For Example:

Turning Point (Direct Appeal) $24.99

A3 Meaningful Letters 9.99

B1 How to Make/ Parole 19.99

Shipping Always Free

Total $54.97

Make Checks Payable To:

Mainline Press LLC

PO Box 517

Creswell, OR 97426

* * * We do not replace lost, damaged, denied, rejected, or stolen guides * *

PROUD
MEMBER

idea INDEX

Incarcerated Dreamers Entrepreneurs Authors

TURNING POINT

VIRTUAL OFFICE SERVICES

The design and layout of this book was performed by Rae
at
Turning Point Virtual Office Services
(a division of Project Mainline)

Do you have a business or personal project that you need help with? Are you writing a book, starting a business, trying to do online dating, searching for pen pals, trying to sell your artwork, wanting to set up or manage your social media pages, in need of reentry information on property management companies or job searches? We can help with that and at a price that is well below the industry standard and in some cases below minimum wage. Prices start at $10 per hour. Imagine what you could get done with someone sitting in front of a computer working only on your project for 8, 10, or 20 hours.

Services:

• Personal Assistant
• Online Research
• Investment Monitoring
• Typing/Word processing
• Song Lyric Searches
• Book Editing/Formatting
• Graphic Design
• Publishing
• Web Design
• Social Media Set-Up & Management
~ Facebook
~ Twitter
~ Instagram
~ LinkedIn
~ Blogs
• Business Management
• Pen Pal Management
and much more!

We offer our services in assisting you with your positive projects. We do not send sexy photos, erotic stories, perform people searches, or help you to profit from your crime. We are here to assist you with positive projects only and reserve the right to refuse services to anyone whom we see fit.

Have your people reach us at:
TPVOS.Main@gmail.com
Or Send a SASE to:
Mainline Press LLC
PO Box 517
Creswell, OR 97426

Made in United States
Cleveland, OH
13 September 2026

44165749R00063